SUBTRACTION FACTS THAT STICK

SUBTRACTION FACTS THAT STICK

Help Your Child Master the Subtraction Facts
for Good in Just Eight Weeks

KATE SNOW

WELL-TRAINED MIND PRESS

TABLE OF CONTENTS

PREFACE

My first job out of college was teaching fifth grade in an excellent public school in the Boston suburbs. I was thrilled to have the chance to work in such a great school district, and I could hardly wait to meet my students as I prepared for my first year of teaching.

Most of all, I was excited to teach math. I majored in math in college, and I eagerly looked forward to sharing my love of the subject with my students. Even before school began, I started to plan lessons covering the usual fifth-grade topics, like geometry, fractions, decimals, and percentages.

However, it only took a couple weeks into the school year for me to realize that some of my students needed a better mastery of the basics before they'd be ready to tackle fifth-grade work. My colleagues in the lower grades assured me that they'd taught the math facts diligently and encouraged parents to work on the facts at home. So why did I have bright ten-year-olds in my class who couldn't subtract 9 from 13?

As I probed further, I discovered that nearly all of my students had once memorized their math facts. But the facts just hadn't stuck. Their teachers and parents had conscientiously made flash cards and drilled the facts, over and over. This method had worked for some of the children. But for others, it seemed that these essential facts had gone straight into short-term memory and then straight out again.

So, instead of repeating a method that hadn't worked, I decided to try a different approach with my students. Instead of using rote memorization to master the facts, I taught my students how to visualize the numbers and use mental strategies to find the solutions. This took a little teaching time at the beginning, but the results were worth it. At first, it took my students a few seconds to apply the strategies. But with a little practice, the strategies became so automatic that my students "just knew" the answers—and became much more confident and successful in their math studies as a result.

That was nearly 15 years ago. Since then, I've taught several years of fifth-grade math classes, written math curricula, tutored students who struggle in math, and begun homeschooling my own children. Through these experiences, I've refined the approach I used with my first class of fifth-graders to create a simple, effective program that will help any child master the subtraction facts—all without flash cards or rote memorization. (Note that it's crucial that your child master the addition facts before tackling subtraction, since many subtraction strategies rely on being able to use "backwards addition." If your child has not yet learned the addition facts, I suggest you have your child work through *Addition Facts That Stick* first and then return to this book.)

Over the years, I've met so many parents who want to help their children master these important math foundations but just aren't sure how to do so effectively. That's why I've written this book. It will guide you step by step as you help your child master the subtraction facts, once and for all, so that they truly stick.

INTRODUCTION

Counting: The biggest obstacle to learning the subtraction facts

Remember when your child first started counting? Like me, you probably beamed with pride as your toddler painstakingly counted the crackers on her plate or the toy trains lined up on the carpet. Counting lays the foundation for understanding numbers, and it's an essential skill for little ones to learn. Then, as children grow, they use their counting skills to help them make sense of more complex math concepts, like subtraction. Counting and taking away objects, counting backwards on fingers, and counting crossed-out pictures all help children begin to understand what subtraction means.

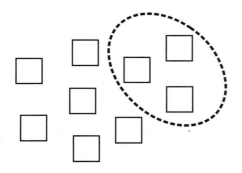

"I had 9 blocks and took away 3 of them."

"I held up 9 fingers and
counted backwards 3."

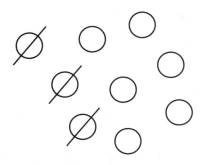

"I drew 9 circles and
crossed out 3."

Three different ways children might use counting to understand 9 – 3.

But although counting helps children *understand the concept* of subtraction, count-ing can actually hold them back and prevent them from *mastering the subtraction facts*. Whether your child is a first-grader tackling the facts for the first time or a fourth-grader who never learned them well, she'll find it hard to become fluent with the sub-traction facts if she relies too much on counting.

Why is counting such a problem?

To understand why counting creates such an obstacle, let's take a closer look at the thought process children use when they count to solve subtraction problems. As an example, imagine a child using blocks to find 12 – 5: First, he counts out 12 blocks. Then, he counts five of the blocks and takes them away. Finally, he counts the remain-ing seven blocks to find the answer.

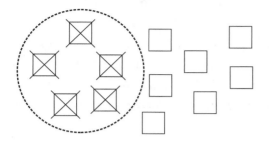

Using blocks to find 12 – 5.

Obviously, this process is slow and inefficient. (Not to mention error-prone: it's easy to make a mistake when you're counting so many blocks!) But even more significantly, this child spends all his mental energy counting and keeping track of blocks. He doesn't have any brain space left over to pay attention to the relationships between the numbers. All he's doing is following a routine procedure, not building a mental framework for knowing the answers automatically.

Instead, children need a way to visualize numbers as *groups*, not collections of single objects that have to be counted. Visualizing numbers as groups allows a child to quickly recall key relationships between numbers (for example, that seven is two more than five, and three less than ten). Then, the child can use those relationships to find answers quickly, without counting. Fortunately, there's a simple tool that allows young learners to visualize numbers as groups: the ten-frame.

The solution: Visualizing numbers on the ten-frame

A ten-frame is a simple grid of ten squares, with a dark line dividing it in half. It may not look like much, but it's a powerful and versatile math tool.

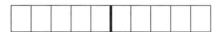

To understand why the ten-frame is so useful, compare these two sets of counters:

You can probably tell right away that there are nine counters on the ten-frame. But can you tell how many counters are in the scattered set without counting one by one?

(Probably not! There are nine in that set as well.) The structure of the ten-frame makes it much easier to recognize and visualize quantities.

The other benefit of the ten-frame is that it reveals important number relationships. The dividing line allows us to immediately see that 9 = 5 + 4, since there are five counters on one side of the line and four counters on the other side. We can also tell straightaway that nine is one less than ten, since there is only one empty box in the ten-frame.

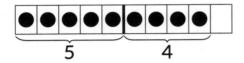

The ten-frame shows that 9 = 5 + 4.

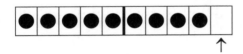

Since only one box is empty, nine must be one less than ten.

Once children learn to visualize numbers as groups on a ten-frame, they can then use their understanding of number relationships to solve subtraction problems efficiently and accurately. For example, to subtract 12 − 5, your child won't need to count out piles of counters or count backwards on her fingers. Instead, she will learn to imagine 12 counters organized on ten-frames.

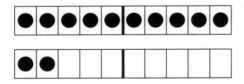

Twelve counters on ten-frames. There are ten on the top ten-frame and two on the bottom ten-frame.

Now, she can simply imagine subtracting five in two steps: First, she visualizes removing two counters from the bottom row. Then, she visualizes removing three counters from the top row (for a total of five counters taken away). Now, it's easy to see that there are seven counters left, so 12 − 5 = 7.

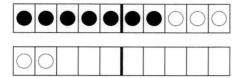

The ten-frame helps children visualize that 12 − 5 = 7.

You'll start by using physical counters on a ten-frame to teach your child how to figure out the answers. As your child becomes more comfortable with the ten-frame, you'll encourage her to begin to imagine it in her head to see the answers without using any actual physical counters. With practice, she'll see the answers so quickly that she'll "just know" the answers and will have the subtraction facts fully mastered.

How to use this book

Instead of overwhelming your child with all 81 subtraction facts, this program breaks the subtraction facts into eight units. Each unit targets a small group of subtraction facts that can be solved with the same mental strategy, and each unit is designed to take about a week. By the end of eight weeks, your child will have learned all the subtraction facts.

In subtraction, the number you're subtracting from (the first number in the problem) is called the minuend. The number you're subtracting (the second number in the problem) is called the subtrahend. The answer to a subtraction problem is called the difference. Your child doesn't need to know these terms, but I will use them sometimes in the instructions for simplicity's sake.

$$7 - 4 = 3$$

minuend   subtrahend   difference

You'll use direct teaching, games, and written practice to help your child master the focus facts for each week. Here's how each week will look:

Day 1: Introduce new facts and teach a new game

On the first day of each week, you will use counters and a ten-frame to help your child learn to visualize numbers. You'll explain a new mental strategy to your child and help your child practice applying the strategy to the week's focus facts. (Don't worry if you have never taught math before—this book will guide you step by step.)

Next, you will teach your child a fun game to practice with the focus facts. These fun games provide a lot of practice in a short amount of time. Even more importantly, they allow you to quickly correct any mistakes and monitor how well your child is using the new mental strategy.

Days 2-5: Play game and complete practice pages

For the rest of the week, you will play the new game again each day. As you play, you'll encourage your child to continue using the mental strategy introduced on Day 1.

Your child will also complete a short practice page each day. This will give your child practice at solving the week's subtraction facts in written form. The practice pages also review all the subtraction facts that your child has learned in previous weeks.

Teaching tips

- Schedule a consistent time each day for subtraction fact practice. You'll be less likely to forget, and your child will be less likely to argue. Try to choose a time when your child is alert and easily able to concentrate.
- Plan to work on the activities in this book for about 15 minutes each session, with five sessions per week. However, different children need different amounts of time to master each group of facts. Feel free to take as long as your child needs to master each unit.
- Discourage your child from counting to solve problems. As discussed above, counting prevents children from understanding the number relationships that lead to subtraction fact mastery. The only exception to this is Week 1, where your child will count back just one or two to solve the −1 and −2 facts.
- Keep the practice sessions positive, upbeat, and fast-paced. Have fun playing the games with your child, and enjoy the one-on-one time together.
- If your child is a reluctant writer, don't let writing difficulties interfere with mastering the subtraction facts. It's fine to have your child answer the worksheet problems orally rather than writing them.
- Many young children freeze when they feel time pressure. Unless your child is age ten or older, don't time him as he does the practice pages. For an older child, aim for your child to know each subtraction fact in three seconds or less.

Is your child ready to master the subtraction facts?

This book is designed for children who understand the concept of subtraction but do not yet know the answers to the subtraction facts automatically. While it's fine to introduce your younger child to the games and strategies, don't expect thorough mastery of the subtraction facts until your child is *at least* seven years old. Subtraction is substantially more difficult for most children than addition, and many children's brains aren't developmentally mature enough to master the subtraction facts until that age.

To be successful at mastering the subtraction facts, your child should first:

- Understand that subtraction can mean taking away or finding a difference. For example, 13 – 7 can mean, "How many are left when you take seven away from 13?" Or, 13 – 7 can be interpreted as, "How much more is 13 than seven?"
- Understand that subtraction is the opposite of addition.
- Know the addition facts up to 9 + 9. Many subtraction strategies rely on being able to use "backwards addition," so this is crucial. (If your child has not yet mastered the addition facts, work through *Addition Facts That Stick* first and then return to this book.)

If your child has these foundational skills in place, she is ready to master the subtraction facts.

What you'll need

All of the game boards and practice pages you'll need for this program are included in the back of the book. You'll also need a few everyday items to complete the activities and play the games:

- 20 small counters of two different colors (tiles, blocks, plastic bears, coins, etc.)
- Coin (any kind with heads and tails)
- Two game tokens
- Deck of regular playing cards
- Regular, six-sided die
- Paper and pencil

WEEK 1

SUBTRACTING ONE AND TWO

WEEK 1 AT A GLANCE

This week, your child will learn to subtract one or two by counting backwards. He'll also learn to recognize quantities on the ten-frame, which will prepare him to master the more difficult subtraction facts in later weeks. Even if your child already knows the −1 and −2 subtraction facts, don't skip this week's ten-frame activities; it's important that he become familiar with this extremely useful way of visualizing numbers.

Week 1 Focus Facts

$2 - 1 = 1$
$3 - 1 = 2$
$4 - 1 = 3$
$5 - 1 = 4$
$6 - 1 = 5$
$7 - 1 = 6$
$8 - 1 = 7$
$9 - 1 = 8$
$10 - 1 = 9$
$3 - 2 = 1$
$4 - 2 = 2$
$5 - 2 = 3$
$6 - 2 = 4$
$7 - 2 = 5$
$8 - 2 = 6$
$9 - 2 = 7$
$10 - 2 = 8$

You will need:

- Ten-frames (page 69)
- Coin
- 20 small counters
- Week 1 Practice Pages (pages 103–109)

DAY 1: NEW TEACHING

Warm-up: Introduce the ten-frame and practice counting backwards

Show your child the ten-frames. Place ten counters on the top ten-frame, as shown.

"How many counters are to the left of the dark line?" *Five.*

"How many counters are to the right of the dark line?" *Five.*

"How many counters are there all together?" *Ten.* If your child isn't sure or starts to count each individual counter, point out that he can add 5 + 5 to find the total.

Remove one counter at a time (starting at the right side) and have your child tell how many counters are left on the ten-frame each time you remove one. Encourage your child to count backwards from ten to determine how many counters are left (rather than counting how many there are by starting at one).

Introduce −1 facts

Place seven counters on the ten-frame.

"How many counters are there?" *Seven.*

"If I subtract one counter, how many will be left?" *Six.*

Have your child remove the counter farthest to the right to check his answer (or to find the answer, if he's not sure).

Point out that he doesn't need to count each counter one by one to figure out how many are left. Since he knows that there were seven counters to start, he can just count backward from seven ("7, 6") to find the new number of counters.

Write **7 −1 =** on a sheet of paper.

"There were seven counters (point to the 7), and then I subtracted one (point to the minus sign and 1). Now there are six counters left. So, seven minus one equals six." Complete the written subtraction problem: 7 − 1 = 6.

Introduce −2 facts

Write **9 − 2 =** on a piece of paper. Ask your child to model the problem with counters. (He should place nine counters on the ten-frame and then remove the two counters farthest to the right.)

"How many counters are left?" *Seven.* If needed, encourage him to count backwards from nine to find the answer: "9, 8, 7."

"So, what's nine minus two?" *Seven.* Have your child complete the written problem: **9 − 2 = 7.**

Have your child use counters to model the other subtraction facts for this week and find their answers. (They are listed on page 18.) Make sure he always fills in the ten-frame from left to right without skipping any boxes and then removes the counters farthest to the right.

Play *Race to 0*

Teach your child to play *Race to 0* and play several times.

MATERIALS

- Ten-frames (page 69)

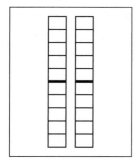

- Coin
- 20 small counters

OBJECT OF THE GAME

Be the first to reach zero.

HOW TO PLAY

Each player chooses a ten-frame and fills it with ten counters.

On your turn, flip the coin. If it is heads, remove one counter from your ten-frame. If it is tails, remove two counters from your ten-frame. Say the matching subtraction fact as you remove the counters. For example, if you have eight counters on your ten-frame and then remove two, say, "Eight minus two equals six."

"8 – 2 = 6."

Then, it is the other player's turn. Continue until one person has removed all the counters from his ten-frame. Keep the game fun and fast-paced.

GAME NOTE

Always remove the counters on the ten-frame in order, from right to left.

Days 2-5: *Race to 0* and Practice Pages

Each day, play *Race to 0* several times.

Also have your child complete one Week 1 Practice Sheet each day. If he gets stuck, encourage him to count backwards from the minuend (the first number in the problem). For example, to figure out seven minus two, he can count backwards two from seven: "7, 6, 5."

Answers to the Practice Pages can be found on page 168.

WEEK 2

SUBTRACTING THREE AND FOUR

WEEK 2 AT A GLANCE

Last week, you taught your child to subtract one or two by removing one or two counters from the ten-frame and counting backwards to find how many counters were left. This week, your child will learn to subtract three and four. She will continue to take away counters from the ten-frame, but she won't count backwards to find the remaining number of counters. Instead, she will use the structure of the ten-frame (especially the dark dividing line in the middle) to figure out how many counters are left.

Week 2 Focus Facts:

$10 - 3 = 7$
$10 - 4 = 6$
$9 - 4 = 5$
$9 - 3 = 6$
$8 - 4 = 4$
$8 - 3 = 5$
$7 - 4 = 3$
$7 - 3 = 4$
$6 - 4 = 2$
$6 - 3 = 3$
$5 - 4 = 1$
$5 - 3 = 2$
$4 - 3 = 1$

You will need:

- Ten-frame cards 1-9 (page 71)
- Ten-frames (page 69)
- Paper and pencil
- 20 small counters of two different colors
- *Tic-Tac-Toe* game board (page 73)
- 6s, 7s, 8s, 9s, and 10s from a deck of cards (four of each, 20 total cards)
- Week 2 Practice Pages (pages 111–117)

DAY 1: NEW TEACHING

Warm-up activity

Show your child the ten-frame card with six circles.

"How many circles are there?" *Six.* Point out that the dark line in the middle divides the ten-frame into groups of five. "So, there are five circles on the left side of the frame, plus one more circle on the right side, for a total of six circles."

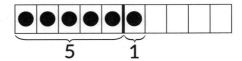

Discuss a couple more cards in this way to make sure your child understands what the cards show.

Shuffle all of the ten-frame cards. Flash each card for a second or two and ask how many circles there are. Adjust your pace to your child, and stop and allow more time to look at a card if needed. Encourage your child to use reasoning—not counting one by one—to figure out how many circles are on each card.

Introduce new facts

Write **10 − 4 =** on a piece of paper and place ten counters on the ten-frame.

"Imagine if I took away four of the counters." Cover the four counters farthest to the right with a blank piece of paper or your hand.

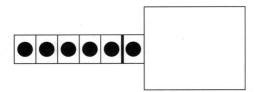

"How many counters would be left?" *Six*. Encourage your child to use reasoning—not counting one by one—to figure out how many counters are left on the ten-frame. Since there are five counters to the left of the dark line and one counter to the right of the dark line, there must be 5 + 1, or six counters.

Have your child complete the written problem: **10 − 4 = 6.**

Write **7 − 3 =** on a piece of paper and place seven counters on the ten-frame.

"Imagine if I took away three of the counters. First, I'd take away the two counters on the right side of the dark line." (Point to these two counters.)

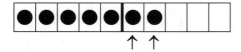

"Then, I'd still need to take away one more counter on the other side of the dark line." (Point to this counter.)

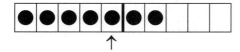

"How many counters would be left then?" *Four*. Have her remove the three counters to confirm her answer.

Have your child complete the written problem: **7 − 3 = 4.**

Have your child use counters to model the other subtraction facts for this week and find their answers. (They are listed on page 24.) Make sure she always fills in the ten-frame from left to right without skipping any boxes, and remind her to use reasoning—not counting—to find the number of counters that are left.

Play *Subtraction Tic-Tac-Toe*

Teach your child how to play *Subtraction Tic-Tac-Toe* and play several times.

MATERIALS

- *Subtraction Tic-Tac-Toe* game board (page 73)

7	4	3
6	5	6
4	3	5

- 6s, 7s, 8s, 9s, and 10s from a regular deck of cards (four each; 20 cards total)
- Five small counters per player, with a different color for each player

OBJECT OF THE GAME

Be the first player to fill three boxes in a row (as in regular *Tic-Tac-Toe*).

HOW TO PLAY

Shuffle the cards and place the stack face down on the table. On your turn, flip over the top card. Subtract either three or four from the card and place one of your counters on the box that matches the difference. For example, if you draw a nine, you can subtract three from nine and place a marker on a box with a six. Or, you can subtract four from nine and place a marker on a box with a five.

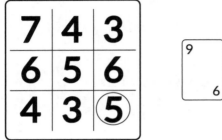

One possible play if you draw a nine. Since 9 – 4 = 5, you can cover a five.

Another possible play if you draw a nine. Since 9 – 3 = 6, you can cover a six.

Play then passes to the other player. Continue until one player has completed an entire row, column, or diagonal.

Days 2-5: *Subtraction Tic-Tac-Toe* and Practice Pages

Each day, play *Subtraction Tic-Tac-Toe* several times. Then, have your child complete one Week 2 Practice Page to practice writing the answers to this week's subtraction facts and to review the facts learned so far. If needed, have her either put counters on the ten-frame or visualize counters to find the answers.

Over the course of the week, encourage your child to gradually transition from actual counters on the ten-frame to imagined counters in her head so that she learns to "see" the answers. Different children will progress at different speeds, but here is a sample of what this might look like:

- Day 2: Child acts out each step of each problem with physical counters.
- Day 3: Child represents the minuends (the first numbers in the problems) with physical counters and then imagines removing the subtrahends (the second numbers in the problems).
- Day 4: Child closes her eyes and visualizes the counters for most problems. She only occasionally uses physical counters for the more difficult problems.
- Day 5: Child solves nearly all the problems without counters.

If your child has trouble visualizing the counters, continue practicing this week's warm-up activity each day. Also have her practice looking at each card, closing her eyes, and then picturing the same arrangement. Remind her to pay close attention to the dark line in the middle of the ten-frame to help her visualize the numbers as groups.

Answers to this week's worksheets are on page 169.

WEEK 3

SUBTRACTING NEIGHBOR NUMBERS

WEEK 3 AT A GLANCE

In Weeks 1 and 2, your child solved the –1, –2, –3, and –4 subtraction facts by taking away a matching number of counters. This week, your child will learn to subtract "neighbor numbers" from each other. Neighbor numbers are pairs of numbers that are only one or two apart, such as ten and nine, or seven and five.

Most children find it difficult to visualize removing more than four counters at a time, and so you will teach your child a different approach for solving these problems: backwards addition. Backwards addition is simply using related addition facts to solve subtraction problems. For example, to solve $8 - 7$, your child will think, "Seven plus what equals eight?" and use the ten-frame as needed to find the answer. He'll continue to use this backwards addition strategy in future weeks as well.

Week 3 Focus Facts

$10 - 9 = 1$
$10 - 8 = 2$
$9 - 8 = 1$
$9 - 7 = 2$
$8 - 7 = 1$
$8 - 6 = 2$
$7 - 6 = 1$
$7 - 5 = 2$
$6 - 5 = 1$
$6 - 4 = 2$
$5 - 4 = 1$

You will need:

- Ten-frame cards 1-9, cut apart on the dotted lines (page 71, optional)
- Ten-frames (page 69)
- Paper and pencil
- 20 small counters, of two different colors
- Two each of the following numbers from a deck of cards: 3, 4, 5, 6, 7, 8, 9 (14 cards total)
- Week 3 Practice Pages (pages 119–125)

DAY 1: NEW TEACHING

Warm-up activity (optional)

If your child has had any trouble recognizing quantities on the ten-frame, flash each ten-frame card for a second or two and ask how many circles there are. Adjust your pace to your child, and stop and allow him more time to look at a card if needed. Encourage your child to use reasoning—not counting one by one—to figure out how many circles are on each card.

Using backwards addition to solve subtraction problems

"There are many different ways to solve subtraction problems. One way is to imagine *taking away* an amount. This is what you did the last two weeks when you subtracted one and two, or three and four."

"But we can also use backwards addition to solve subtraction problems. I'll show you what I mean."

Write **8 – 7 =** on a sheet of paper.

"To find eight minus seven, you could put eight counters on the ten-frame and then take seven away. But it can be hard to visualize taking away so many counters. To solve problems like this one, it's easier to think about subtraction in a different way. Subtraction can also mean *how many more*. So, eight minus seven means 'Seven plus how many more is eight?'"

Write **7 + ____ = 8** below **8 – 7 =** on the sheet of paper.

Place seven counters on the ten-frame.

33

"How many more counters do we need to have eight?" *One.* Add one counter of another color to the ten-frame for a total of eight. Have your child complete the addition problem: **7 +_1_ = 8.**

"Since seven plus one equals eight, eight is one more than seven. So, eight minus seven equals one." Have your child complete the written subtraction problem: **8 – 7 = 1.**

Introduce new facts

"Eight and seven are neighbor numbers, because eight and seven are right next to each other in the counting sequence. Can you tell me a neighbor number that's right next to five?" *Four or six.* "Can you tell me another pair of neighbor numbers that are right next to each other?" *Sample answer: Nine and eight.*

"Let's practice another neighbor-number subtraction fact."

Write **10 – 9 =** on a sheet of paper.

"How could you use backwards addition to solve this problem?" *I could think, 'Nine plus what equals ten?'*

Write **9 + ___ = 10** below **10 – 9 =** on the sheet of paper.

Place nine counters on the ten-frame.

"Nine plus how many more counters equals ten?" *One.* Have your child add one counter of another color to show that nine plus one equals ten. Have him complete the addition problem: **9 + _1_ = 10.**

"So, what does ten minus nine equal?" *One.* Have your child complete the written subtraction problem: **10 – 9 = 1.**

"Neighbor numbers don't have to be right next to each other. Neighbors can also live two doors down from each other, so neighbor numbers can also be two numbers apart, like five and seven. Can you name another pair of neighbor numbers that are two apart?" *Sample answer: Two and four.*

Write **7 – 5** on a sheet of paper.

"How could you use backwards addition to solve this problem?" *I could think, 'Five plus what equals seven?'*

Write **5 + ___ = 7** below **7 – 5 =** on the sheet of paper.

Place five counters on the ten-frame.

"Think about what seven looks like on the ten-frame. Five plus how many more counters equals seven?" *Two.* Have your child add two counters of another counter to show that five plus two equals seven. Have him complete the addition problem: **5 + _2_ = 7.**

"So, what does seven minus five equal?" *Two.* Have your child complete the written subtraction problem: **7 – 5 = 2.**

Repeat this process for this week's other subtraction facts. (They are listed on page 32.) Write the matching addition fact for each subtraction fact, since this will help your child remember to use backwards addition to find the answers. If your child readily knows the answers to these problems, you do not need to model every one on the ten-frame.

(Note: Your child might wonder if numbers that are three or four apart are also neighbor numbers. I limit neighbor numbers to pairs that are one or two apart because there are other strategies that are more useful once the numbers are farther apart. "Neighbor number" is simply a convenient way to think about these subtraction facts and not a real math term.)

Play *Neighbor Number Memory*

Teach your child how to play *Neighbor Number Memory* and play a couple of times.

MATERIALS

- Two each of the following numbers from a deck of cards: 3, 4, 5, 6, 7, 8, 9 (14 cards total)

OBJECT OF THE GAME

Collect the most pairs of cards.

HOW TO PLAY

Shuffle the cards together and place them face-down in a grid.

On your turn, flip over two cards. If the cards have a difference of one or two, state the matching subtraction fact and keep the cards. For example, if you turn over a seven and a six, say, "Seven minus six equals one." Or, if you turn over a five and a three, say, "Five minus three equals two." If the cards do not have a difference of one or two, turn them back over.

Take turns until you cannot match any more cards. (There may be a few left over.) Whoever has found more pairs wins.

Days 2–5: *Neighbor Number Memory* and Practice Pages

Each day, play *Neighbor Number Memory*. Then, have your child complete one of the Week 3 Practice Pages. As he works, remind him to use backwards addition and to either put counters on the ten-frame or visualize counters to find the answers.

Over the course of the week, encourage your child to gradually transition from actual counters on the ten-frame to imagined counters in his head so that he learns to "see" the answers. Different children will progress at different speeds, but here is a sample of what this might look like:

- Day 2: Child acts out each step of each backwards addition problem with physical counters.
- Day 3: Child represents the first number in each backwards addition problem with counters and then visualizes the missing addend.
- Day 4: Child visualizes the counters for most problems. He only occasionally uses physical counters for the more difficult problems.
- Day 5: Child solves nearly all the problems without counters.

Answers to this week's Practice Pages are on page 170.

WEEK 4

SUBTRACTING FIVE, SIX, AND SEVEN

WEEK 4 AT A GLANCE

This week, your child will finish learning the subtraction facts in which the minuend (the first number in the subtraction problem) is ten or less. She'll continue to use backwards addition to find the answers to this week's subtraction facts.

Week 4 Focus Facts:

10 – 7 = 3
10 – 6 = 4
10 – 5 = 5
9 – 6 = 3
9 – 5 = 4
8 – 5 = 3

You will need:

- Ten-frames (page 69)
- Paper and pencil
- 20 small counters of two different colors
- Two *Climb to the Top* game boards (one for each player, pages 75 and 77)
- 5s, 6s, 7s, 8s, 9s, and 10s from a deck of cards (four of each; 24 cards total)
- Week 4 Practice Pages (pages 127–133)

DAY 1: NEW TEACHING

Introduce new facts

Write **9 − 6 =** on a piece of paper and place six counters on the ten-frame.

"You learned last week how to use backwards addition to solve subtraction problems. We're going to keep using backwards addition this week. So, to find nine minus six, think, 'Six plus what equals nine?' "

Write **6 + ___ = 9** below **9 − 6 =** on the sheet of paper.

"Let's figure out how many more counters we need to reach nine."

Have your child point to the last box that would need to be filled for there to be nine counters.

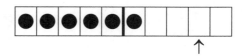

Then, have her add counters of a different color until there are a total of nine counters on the ten-frame.

"How many counters did you add to reach nine?" *Three.*

"So, six plus what equals nine?" *Three.*

Have your child complete the written addition problem: **6 +_3_ = 9.**

"If six plus three equals nine, what does nine minus six equal?" *Three.*

Have your child complete the written problem: **9 − 6 = 3.**

Repeat with the other subtraction facts for this week. (They are listed on page 38.) As in the example above, have your child model each problem with counters and use backwards addition to find the answers.

Play *Climb to the Top*

Teach your child how to play *Climb to the Top* and play several times.

MATERIALS

- Two *Climb to the Top* game boards (pages X-X)

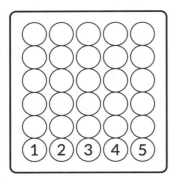 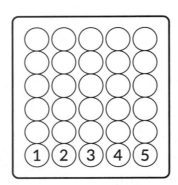

- 5s, 6s, 7s, 8s, 9s, and 10s from a regular deck of cards (four each; 24 cards total)
- 20 small counters per player

OBJECT OF THE GAME

Be the first player to fill in an entire column and reach the top of the game board.

HOW TO PLAY

Shuffle the cards and place the stack face down on the table. On your turn, flip over the top two cards. Subtract the smaller number from the larger number to find the difference between the two cards. Place a counter on the lowest empty box in the column that matches the difference.

For example, if you draw a nine and a five, place a counter in the box above the four, since 9 − 5 = 4.

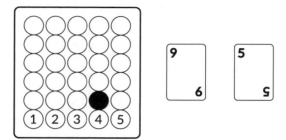

If the two cards are the same, you may place the counter in any column.

Play then passes to the other player. Continue until one player has filled in an entire column and reached the top.

As you play, continue to encourage your child to use backwards addition to find the differences. Also allow her to construct the problems on the ten-frame as needed.

GAME NOTE

This game also reviews the neighbor-number subtraction facts that your child learned in Week 3.

Days 2-5: *Climb to the Top* and Practice Pages

Each day, play *Climb to the Top* several times. Then, have your child complete one Week 4 Practice Page to practice writing the answers to this week's subtraction facts and to review facts learned so far. As she works, remind her to use backwards addition and to either put counters on the ten-frame or visualize counters to find the answers. Over the course of the week, encourage her to gradually transition from actual counters on the ten-frame to imagined counters in her head so that she learns to "see" the answers.

Answers to this week's worksheets are on page 171.

WEEK 5

SUBTRACTING NINE

WEEK 5 AT A GLANCE

Now that your child has learned all of the subtraction facts in which the minuend (the first number) is ten or less, he will begin subtracting from numbers greater than ten. He'll begin to use two ten-frames to model these larger minuends.

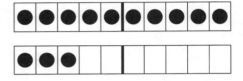

Modeling 13 on two ten-frames.

Just as the dividing line in the middle of the ten-frame helps children visualize the numbers up to ten, the jump from one ten-frame to another ten-frame provides an important visual benchmark for solving problems when the minuend is greater than ten.

This week, your child will use backwards addition to solve the –9 facts. He'll use the jump between ten-frames to help him add up to find the answers. You'll teach him to add up in two steps to make it easier.

This week, your child will learn these new facts:

$11 - 9 = 2$
$12 - 9 = 3$
$13 - 9 = 4$
$14 - 9 = 5$
$15 - 9 = 6$
$16 - 9 = 7$
$17 - 9 = 8$
$18 - 9 = 9$

You will need:

- Ten-frame Cards 10-18 (page 79), cut apart on the dotted lines
- Ten-frames (page 69)
- 20 small counters of two different colors
- *Subtracting Nines* game boards, edges trimmed and placed side by side to make one continuous game board (pages 83 and 85)
- Number Cards, cut apart on the dotted lines (page 81)
- Two game tokens
- Week 5 Practice Pages (pages 135–141)

DAY 1: NEW TEACHING

Warm-up activity

Show your child the ten-frame card for 14.

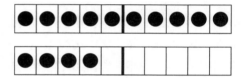

"How many circles are there?" *14.* If he's not sure, point out that there is an entire row of ten, plus four more. Encourage him to use his understanding of place-value to figure out that there are 14 circles (rather than counting one by one).

Discuss a couple more cards in this way to make sure your child understands what the cards show.

Shuffle all of the ten-frame cards. Flash each card for a second or two and ask how many circles there are. Adjust your pace to your child, and stop and allow more time to look at a card if needed.

Introduce new facts

Write **13 – 9 =** on a sheet of paper.

"How could you use backwards addition to solve this problem?" *I could think "Nine plus what equals 13?"*

Write **9 + ___ = 13** below **13 – 9 =** on the sheet of paper.

Place nine counters on the top ten-frame.

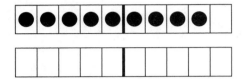

"Let's figure out how many more counters we need to reach 13."

Have your child point to the last box that would need to be filled for there to be 13 counters.

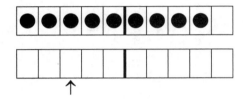

Then, have him add counters of a different color until there are a total of 13 counters on the ten-frames. Encourage your child to think about adding the counters in two steps: First, have him find how many counters it takes to fill in the top ten-frame (one).

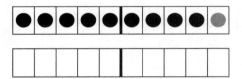

Then, have him figure out how many more counters are needed on the bottom ten-frame to reach 13 (three more).

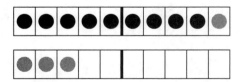

"Nine plus what equals 13?" *Four.* Have him complete the written addition problem: **9 +_4_ = 13.**

"So, what does 13 minus nine equal?" *Four.* Have your child complete the written subtraction problem: **13 − 9 = 4.**

Repeat for this week's other subtraction facts. (They are listed on page 44.) As in the example above, have your child model each problem with counters and use backwards addition to find the answers.

Play *Subtracting Nines*

Teach your child how to play *Subtracting Nines* and play several times.

MATERIALS

- *Subtracting Nines* game boards, edges trimmed and placed side by side to make one continuous game board (pages 83 and 85)

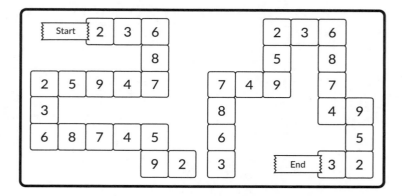

- Number Cards, cut apart on the dotted lines (page 81)
- Game token for each player

OBJECT OF THE GAME

Be the first player to reach the end of the game board.

HOW TO PLAY

Shuffle the Number Cards and place them face down in a pile. Place each player's game token on Start.

To play, turn over the top card in the pile. Subtract nine from the number and then advance your token to the next space with that number. For example, if you turn over a 16, advance your token to the next seven, since 16 − 9 = 7. Play then passes to the other player. Continue until one of you reaches the end of the path.

Allow your child to construct the numbers on the ten-frame if necessary, and encourage him to use backwards addition to find the answers.

Days 2-5: *Subtracting Nines* and Practice Pages

Each day, play *Subtracting Nines* several times. Then, have your child complete one Week 5 Practice Page to practice writing the answers to this week's subtraction facts and to review facts learned so far. As he works, remind him to use backwards addition and to either put counters on the ten-frame or visualize counters to find the answers. Over the course of the week, encourage him to gradually transition from actual counters on the ten-frame to imagined counters in his head so that he learns to "see" the answers.

Answers to this week's worksheets are on page 172.

WEEK 6

SUBTRACTING EIGHT

WEEK 6 AT A GLANCE

This week's lesson is very similar to Week 5. Your child will continue to use backwards addition as she finds answers to the −8 facts on two ten-frames. She'll add up in two steps to make the adding easier.

This week, your child will learn these new facts:

$11 - 8 = 3$
$12 - 8 = 4$
$13 - 8 = 5$
$14 - 8 = 6$
$15 - 8 = 7$
$16 - 8 = 8$
$17 - 8 = 9$

You will need:

- Ten-frame Cards 10-18 (page 79)
- Ten-frames (page 69)
- 20 counters of two different colors
- Two *Subtracting Eights Bingo* game boards (one for each player, pages 89 and 91)
- Number Cards, cut apart on the dotted lines (page 87)
- Week 6 Practice Pages (pages 143–149)

DAY 1: NEW TEACHING

Warm-up activity

If your child had any trouble recognizing the numbers greater than ten on ten-frames last week, flash each ten-frame card for a second or two and ask how many counters there are.

Introduce new facts

Write **14 − 8 =** on a sheet of paper.

"How could you use backwards addition to solve this problem?" *I could think "Eight plus what equals 14?"*

Write **8 + ___ = 14** below **14 − 8 =** .

Place eight counters on the top ten-frame.

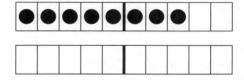

"Let's figure out how many more counters we need to reach 14."

Have your child point to the last box that would need to be filled for there to be 14 counters.

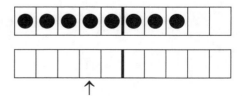

51

Then, have her add counters of a different color until there are a total of 14 counters on the ten-frames. Encourage your child to think about adding the counters in two steps: First, have her find how many counters it takes to fill in the top ten-frame (two).

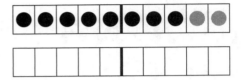

Then, have her figure out how many more counters are needed on the bottom ten-frame to reach 14 (four more).

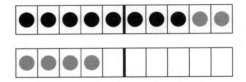

"So, eight plus what equals 14?" *Six.* Have her complete the written addition problem: **8 +_6_ = 14.**

"What does 14 minus eight equal?" *Six.* Have your child complete the written subtraction problem: **14 – 8 = 6.**

Repeat for this week's other subtraction facts. (They are listed on page X.) As in the example above, have your child model each problem with counters and use backwards addition to find the answers.

Play *Subtracting Eights Bingo*

Teach your child how to play *Subtracting Eights Bingo* and play several times.

MATERIALS

- Two *Subtracting Eights Bingo* game boards (one for each player, pages 89 and 91)

9	8	3	5	4
7	6	9	3	8
4	5	FREE	6	5
5	6	8	9	3
9	4	3	7	6

3	4	9	6	8
7	5	9	3	4
8	6	FREE	7	6
6	5	4	3	9
3	7	9	8	5

- Number Cards 11–18, cut apart on the dotted lines (page 87)
- 20 small counters per player

OBJECT OF THE GAME

Be the first player to fill the boxes in an entire column, row, or diagonal.

HOW TO PLAY

This game is like traditional *Bingo*, with your child as the "caller."

Give each player a game board and counters. Shuffle the cards and place them face down in a pile.

Have your child turn over the top card and subtract eight from the number on the card. Then, each of you uses a counter to cover a square containing the answer on your own game board. For example, if the card is a 15, your child says, "15 minus eight equals seven," and both of you cover a seven.

9	8	3	5	4
(7)	6	9	3	8
4	5	FREE	6	5
5	6	8	9	3
9	4	3	7	6

3	4	9	6	8
7	5	9	3	4
8	6	FREE	(7)	6
6	5	4	3	9
3	7	9	8	5

Continue until one of you wins by filling an entire column, row, or diagonal. When you run out of number cards, simply shuffle the stack and keep playing. As you play, encourage your child to visualize the subtraction problems on the ten-frame and allow her to model them with counters if needed.

Days 2-5: *Subtracting Eights Bingo* and Practice Pages

Each day, play *Subtracting Eights Bingo* several times. Then, have your child complete one Week 6 Practice Sheet. As she works, remind her to use backwards addition and to either put counters on the ten-frame or visualize counters to find the answers. Over the course of the week, encourage her to gradually transition from actual counters on the ten-frame to imagined counters in her head so that she learns to "see" the answers.

Answers to this week's worksheets are on page 173.

SUBTRACTING THREE, FOUR, AND FIVE FROM NUMBERS GREATER THAN TEN

WEEK 7 AT A GLANCE

Your child will remove counters to subtract three, four, and five from numbers greater than ten this week. You'll teach him to remove the counters in two steps so that he can continue to use the jump between ten-frames as a benchmark for visualizing these problems. For example, to solve 12 – 3, he'll first take away two counters (to get to ten), and then take one counter away from ten to find that the answer is nine.

This week, your child will learn these new facts:

$14 - 5 = 9$
$13 - 5 = 8$
$12 - 5 = 7$
$11 - 5 = 6$
$13 - 4 = 9$
$12 - 4 = 8$
$11 - 4 = 7$
$12 - 3 = 9$
$11 - 3 = 8$
$11 - 2 = 9$

You will need:

- Ten-frames (page 69)
- 20 counters of two different colors
- Two *Roll and Cover* game boards (pages 93 and 95)
- Regular, six-sided die
- Week 7 Practice Pages (pages 151–157)

DAY 1: NEW TEACHING

Introduce new facts

Write **14 – 5 =** on a sheet of paper. Place 14 counters on the ten-frames.

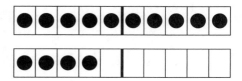

"To subtract five from 14, we'll take away five counters. We'll do it in two steps."
"First, I take away all the counters on the bottom ten-frame." Remove the four counters on the bottom ten-frame.

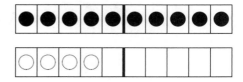

"How many more counters do I need to remove?" *One, since four plus one is five.* Remove one more counter.

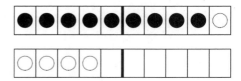

"So, what is 14 minus five?" *Nine.*

Complete the written subtraction problem: **14 – 5 = 9.**

Repeat for this week's other subtraction facts. (They are listed on page 56.) Each time, encourage your child to first remove the counters on the bottom ten-frame and then figure out how many more he needs to take away on the top ten-frame.

NOTE

Some children prefer to solve these subtraction problems with backwards addition rather than using the "take-away" strategy. As long as your child can solve the problems efficiently and reliably, he can use whichever approach makes the most sense to him.

Play *Roll and Cover*

Teach your child how to play *Roll and Cover* and play several times.

MATERIALS

- 20 counters of two different colors
- Two *Roll and Cover* game boards (pages 93 and 95)

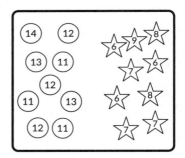 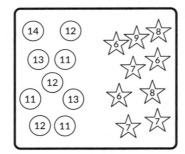

- Regular, six-sided die

OBJECT OF THE GAME

Cover all the spaces on your game board before the other player.

HOW TO PLAY

On your turn, roll the die. Use the number you rolled to create a subtraction problem with a number in a star and a number in a circle, so that that the circled number minus the number showing on the die equals the starred number. Cover the circled number and starred number with counters.

Create a subtraction problem so that the circled number minus the number of dots on the die equals the starred number.

For example, if you roll a three, you might choose a circled 12 from the left side of the board and a starred nine from the right side, since 12 – 3 = 9. Or, you could choose to cover a circled 11 and a starred eight, since 11 – 3 = 8.

Ones are wild; if you roll a one, you may cover any one circled number and one starred number. Take turns with your child. The first player to cover all the circles and stars on his game board wins.

Days 2-5: *Roll and Cover* and Practice Pages

Each day, play *Roll and Cover* several times. Then, have your child complete one Week 7 Practice Sheet to practice writing the answers to this week's subtraction facts and to review facts learned so far. As he works, remind him to use backwards addition and to either put counters on the ten-frame or visualize counters to find the answers. Over the course of the week, encourage him to gradually transition from actual counters on the ten-frame to imagined counters in his head so that he learns to "see" the answers.

Answers to this week's worksheets are on page 174.

WEEK 8

SUBTRACTING SIX AND SEVEN FROM NUMBERS GREATER THAN 10

WEEK 8 AT A GLANCE

Your child will finish mastering the subtraction facts as she learns to subtract six and seven from numbers greater than ten this week. For these subtraction facts, some children prefer to imagine taking away counters, while others prefer using backwards addition. You'll demonstrate both approaches in the lesson this week, and then your child can use whichever method feels more comfortable to her.

This week, your child will learn these new facts:

$16 - 7 = 9$
$15 - 7 = 8$
$14 - 7 = 7$
$13 - 7 = 6$
$12 - 7 = 5$
$11 - 7 = 4$
$15 - 6 = 9$
$14 - 6 = 8$
$13 - 6 = 7$
$12 - 6 = 6$
$11 - 6 = 5$

You will need:

- Ten-frames (page 69)
- 20 counters of two different colors
- *Subtraction Crash* game board (page 97)
- *Subtraction Crash* game cards, cut apart on the dotted lines (page 99)
- Week 8 Practice Pages (pages 159–165)

DAY 1: NEW TEACHING

Introduce new facts

Write **14 – 7 =** on a sheet of paper.

"Some kids like to imagine taking away counters for subtraction facts like this one, and some kids like to use backwards addition to solve it. Both ways work well for this week's facts. I'm going to show you both ways and then you can decide which way feels more comfortable for you."

Place 14 counters on the ten-frames.

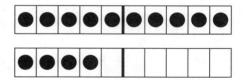

"Let's try removing seven counters first. We'll do it in two steps again, just like last week. First, I take away all the counters on the bottom ten-frame." Remove the four counters on the bottom ten-frame.

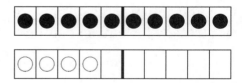

"How many more counters do I need to remove?" *Three, since four plus three is seven.* Remove three more counters.

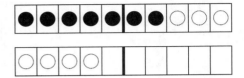

"So, what is 14 minus seven?" *Seven*.

Complete the written subtraction problem: **14 – 7 = 7.**

"You could also solve this problem with backwards addition."

Place seven counters on the top ten-frame.

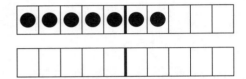

"How many more counters do we need to have 14?" *Seven*. Encourage your child to think about how many counters it takes to fill in the top ten-frame (three), and then how many more are needed on the bottom ten-frame (four).

Have your child add seven counters of a different color to the ten-frames to demonstrate the answer.

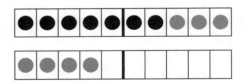

"So, seven plus what equals 14?" *Seven*.

"So, that's another way to figure out that 14 minus seven equals seven."

Have your child find the answers for this week's other subtraction facts. (They are listed on page 62.) Encourage your child to use whichever strategy feels most comfortable to her.

Play *Subtraction Crash*

Teach your child how to play *Subtraction Crash* and play several times.

MATERIALS

- *Subtraction Crash* game board (page 97)

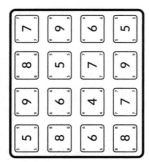

- *Subtraction Crash* game cards, cut apart on the lines (page 99)
- Five counters of two different colors (ten counters total)

OBJECT OF THE GAME

Place five counters on the game board.

HOW TO PLAY

Shuffle the cards and place them face down in a pile. Give one player five counters of one color and the other player five counters of a different color.

On your turn, flip over the top card. Find the answer to the subtraction problem and place a counter on a matching square. For example, if the card says "15 – 7," place a counter on an eight. For the wild card, you may place a counter on any square.

If the other player already has a counter on a number that matches your card, you can "crash" into their counter, remove it, and place your own counter on the number.

Take turns with your child. Whoever places all five of her counters first wins.

Days 2-5: *Subtraction Crash* and Practice Pages

Each day, play *Subtraction Crash* several times. Then, have your child complete one Week 8 Practice Sheet to practice writing the answers to this week's subtraction facts and to review facts learned so far. As she works, remind her to either put counters on the ten-frame or visualize counters to find the answers. Over the course of the week, encourage her to gradually transition from actual counters on the ten-frame to imagined counters in her head so that she learns to "see" the answers.

Answers to this week's worksheets are on page 175.

Congratulations!

Your child has now learned to visualize numbers and find answers for all of the subtraction facts! I hope you and your child have enjoyed the games and activities, and that you'll take some time to celebrate your child's accomplishment (and your own hard work, too!)

If your child cannot recall all of the facts automatically yet, continue playing the games and reminding her to use the "take-away" and "backwards addition" strategies as you play. It's also fine to simply go back through the entire book and review all the units if you find that your child isn't fluent with the subtraction facts yet. Some children simply need a little more practice before they know all the facts with ease. The subtraction facts are essential building blocks for success and confidence in math, so don't be afraid to spend as long as you need on them until they really stick for your child.

GAME BOARDS

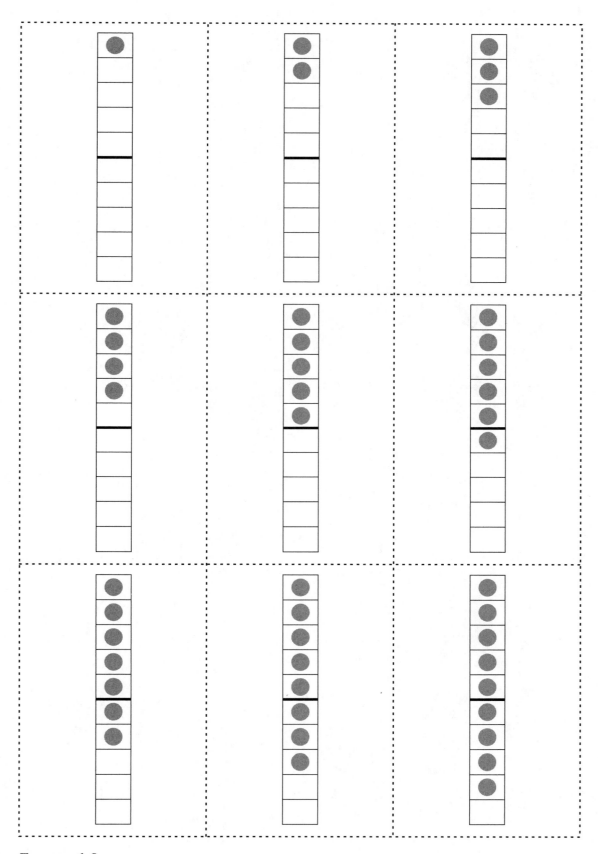

Ten-Frames 1-9

Tic-Tac-Toe

7	4	3
6	5	6
4	3	5

Climb to the Top

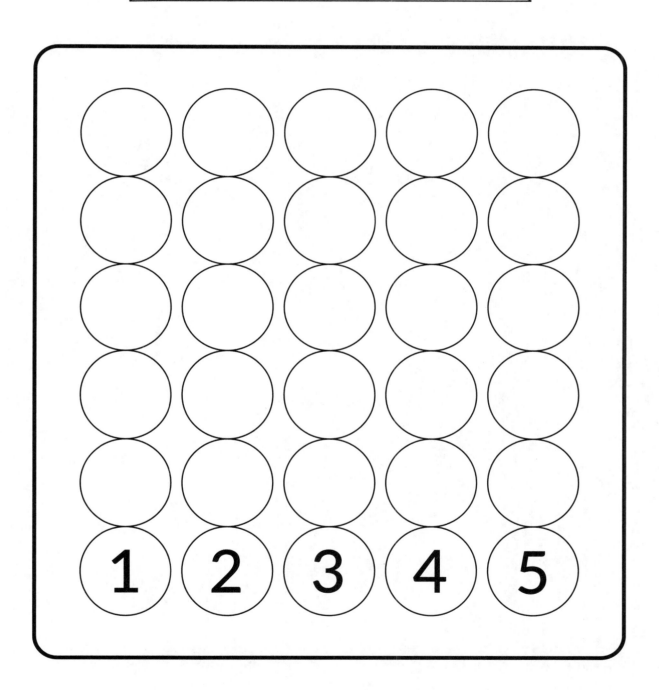

Climb to the Top

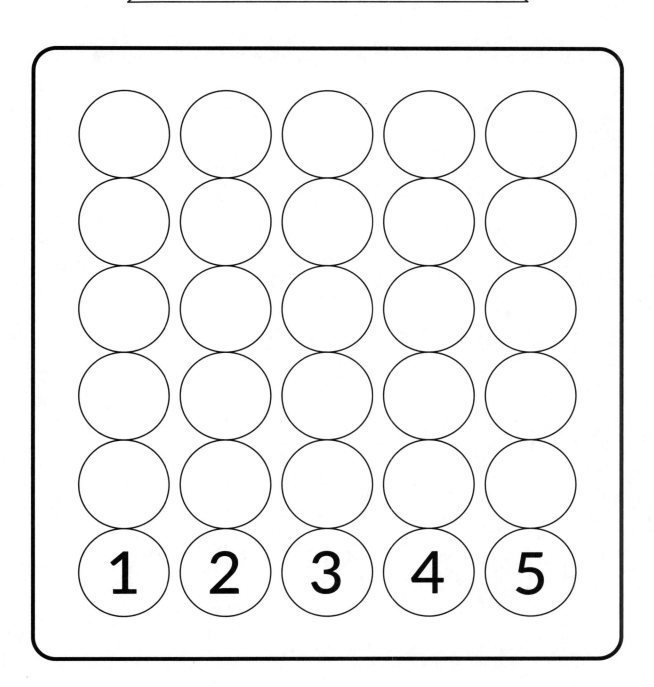

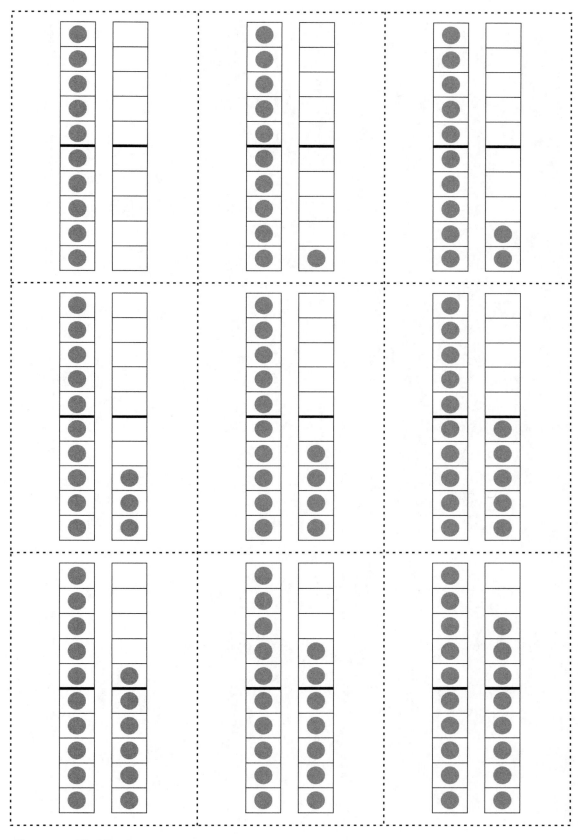

Ten-Frames 10-18

11	12	13
14	15	16
17	18	

Number Cards

Subtracting

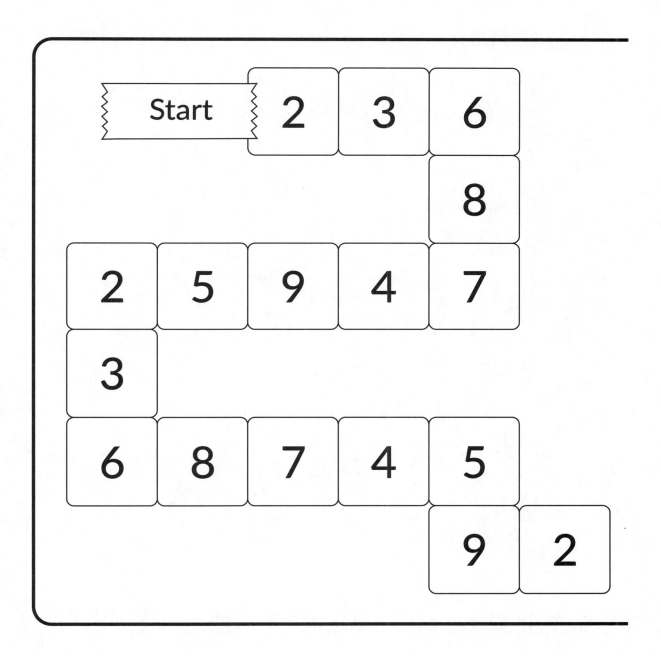

Start | 2 | 3 | 6
8
2 | 5 | 9 | 4 | 7
3
6 | 8 | 7 | 4 | 5
9 | 2

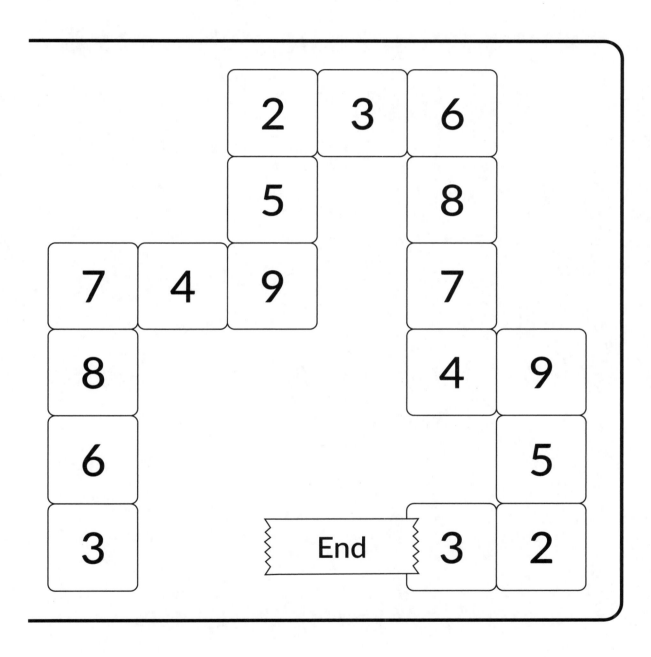

Nines

11	12	13
11	12	13
14	15	16
14	15	16
17	18	
17	18	

Number Cards

Subtracting Eights Bingo

9	8	3	5	4
7	6	9	3	8
4	5	FREE	6	5
5	6	8	9	3
9	4	3	7	6

Subtracting Eights Bingo

3	4	9	6	8
7	5	9	3	4
8	6	FREE	7	6
6	5	4	3	9
3	7	9	8	5

Roll and Cover

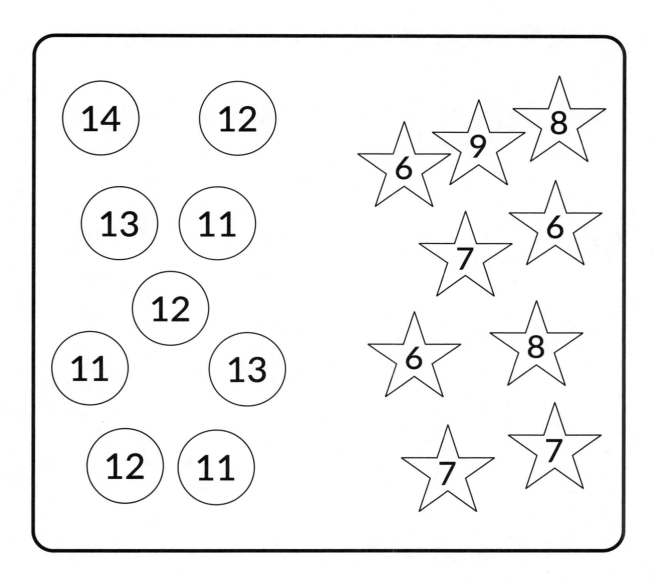

Roll and Cover

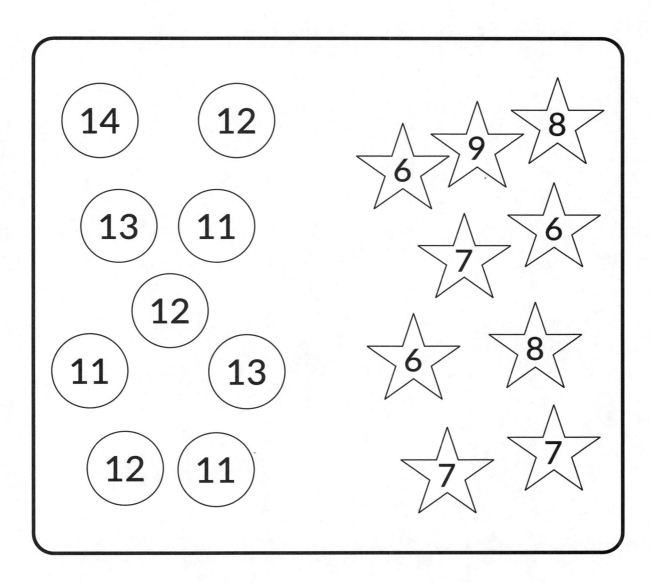

Subtraction Crash

16 – 7	15 – 6
15 – 7	14 – 6
14 – 7	13 – 6
13 – 7	12 – 6
12 – 7	11 – 6
11 – 7	WILD

PRACTICE PAGES

Week 1   ## Practice Page 1

$9 - 2 =$ _____ $4 - 1 =$ _____ $6 - 1 =$ _____

$5 - 2 =$ _____ $7 - 1 =$ _____ $6 - 2 =$ _____

$10 - 1 =$ _____ $3 - 1 =$ _____ $9 - 2 =$ _____

$5 - 1 =$ _____ $7 - 2 =$ _____ $8 - 1 =$ _____

$8 - 2 =$ _____ $3 - 2 =$ _____ $2 - 1 =$ _____

$4 - 2 =$ _____ $9 - 1 =$ _____ $10 - 2 =$ _____

Week 1

Practice Page 2

$9 - 2 = $ _____ $4 - 1 = $ _____ $6 - 1 = $ _____

$7 - 1 = $ _____ $5 - 2 = $ _____ $6 - 2 = $ _____

$3 - 1 = $ _____ $10 - 1 = $ _____ $9 - 2 = $ _____

$7 - 2 = $ _____ $5 - 1 = $ _____ $8 - 1 = $ _____

$3 - 2 = $ _____ $8 - 2 = $ _____ $2 - 1 = $ _____

$9 - 1 = $ _____ $4 - 2 = $ _____ $10 - 2 = $ _____

Week 1 **Practice Page 3**

3 − 1 = _____   10 − 1 = _____   9 − 2 = _____

7 − 2 = _____   5 − 1 = _____   8 − 1 = _____

3 − 2 = _____   8 − 2 = _____   2 − 1 = _____

9 − 1 = _____   4 − 2 = _____   10 − 2 = _____

9 − 2 = _____   4 − 1 = _____   6 − 1 = _____

7 − 1 = _____   5 − 2 = _____   6 − 2 = _____

Week 1

Practice Page 4

10 − 1 = _____   3 − 1 = _____   9 − 2 = _____

5 − 1 = _____   7 − 2 = _____   8 − 1 = _____

8 − 2 = _____   3 − 2 = _____   2 − 1 = _____

4 − 2 = _____   9 − 1 = _____   10 − 2 = _____

4 − 1 = _____   9 − 2 = _____   6 − 1 = _____

5 − 2 = _____   7 − 1 = _____   6 − 2 = _____

Week 2   ## Practice Page 1

$8 - 3 =$ _____ $3 - 2 =$ _____ $9 - 4 =$ _____

$2 - 1 =$ _____ $7 - 3 =$ _____ $9 - 1 =$ _____

$5 - 2 =$ _____ $10 - 3 =$ _____ $8 - 2 =$ _____

$8 - 4 =$ _____ $8 - 2 =$ _____ $3 - 1 =$ _____

$7 - 2 =$ _____ $7 - 4 =$ _____ $9 - 3 =$ _____

$10 - 4 =$ _____ $6 - 1 =$ _____ $6 - 3 =$ _____

Week 2   **Practice Page 2**

$8 - 4 =$ _____ $9 - 2 =$ _____ $8 - 1 =$ _____

$10 - 2 =$ _____ $7 - 4 =$ _____ $9 - 3 =$ _____

$10 - 4 =$ _____ $5 - 1 =$ _____ $6 - 3 =$ _____

$8 - 3 =$ _____ $6 - 2 =$ _____ $9 - 4 =$ _____

$4 - 2 =$ _____ $7 - 3 =$ _____ $10 - 1 =$ _____

$4 - 1 =$ _____ $10 - 3 =$ _____ $7 - 1 =$ _____

Week 2 Practice Page 3

10 − 1 = _____   8 − 2 = _____   8 − 4 = _____

7 − 4 = _____   9 − 3 = _____   3 − 1 = _____

4 − 2 = _____   6 − 3 = _____   10 − 4 = _____

6 − 1 = _____   9 − 4 = _____   8 − 3 = _____

7 − 3 = _____   7 − 2 = _____   5 − 2 = _____

10 − 3 = _____   7 − 1 = _____   9 − 2 = _____

Week 2   **Practice Page 4**

$10 - 2 =$ _____ $6 - 3 =$ _____ $10 - 4 =$ _____

$5 - 1 =$ _____ $9 - 4 =$ _____ $8 - 3 =$ _____

$9 - 1 =$ _____ $6 - 2 =$ _____ $8 - 4 =$ _____

$7 - 4 =$ _____ $9 - 3 =$ _____ $7 - 2 =$ _____

$7 - 3 =$ _____ $2 - 1 =$ _____ $4 - 1 =$ _____

$10 - 3 =$ _____ $8 - 1 =$ _____ $3 - 2 =$ _____

Week 3   **Practice Page 1**

$6 - 5 =$ _____ $8 - 6 =$ _____ $10 - 8 =$ _____

$9 - 7 =$ _____ $10 - 2 =$ _____ $5 - 3 =$ _____

$5 - 2 =$ _____ $7 - 5 =$ _____ $9 - 3 =$ _____

$7 - 6 =$ _____ $8 - 3 =$ _____ $6 - 4 =$ _____

$10 - 3 =$ _____ $10 - 9 =$ _____ $4 - 3 =$ _____

$9 - 8 =$ _____ $7 - 3 =$ _____ $4 - 1 =$ _____

$5 - 4 =$ _____ $8 - 1 =$ _____ $8 - 7 =$ _____

Week 3   **Practice Page 2**

10 − 8 = _____   6 − 5 = _____   8 − 6 = _____

5 − 3 = _____   9 − 7 = _____   7 − 4 = _____

6 − 2 = _____   9 − 4 = _____   7 − 5 = _____

6 − 4 = _____   7 − 6 = _____   7 − 1 = _____

4 − 3 = _____   9 − 2 = _____   10 − 9 = _____

10 − 4 = _____   9 − 8 = _____   8 − 4 = _____

8 − 7 = _____   5 − 4 = _____   6 − 3 = _____

Week 3   Practice Page 3

$4 - 3 =$ _____ $6 - 3 =$ _____ $10 - 9 =$ _____

$7 - 4 =$ _____ $9 - 8 =$ _____ $9 - 4 =$ _____

$8 - 7 =$ _____ $5 - 4 =$ _____ $8 - 2 =$ _____

$10 - 8 =$ _____ $6 - 5 =$ _____ $8 - 6 =$ _____

$5 - 3 =$ _____ $9 - 7 =$ _____ $5 - 1 =$ _____

$9 - 1 =$ _____ $8 - 3 =$ _____ $7 - 5 =$ _____

$6 - 4 =$ _____ $7 - 6 =$ _____ $10 - 4 =$ _____

Week 3   **Practice Page 4**

$6 - 4 =$ _____ $7 - 6 =$ _____ $4 - 2 =$ _____

$4 - 3 =$ _____ $7 - 3 =$ _____ $10 - 9 =$ _____

$9 - 3 =$ _____ $9 - 8 =$ _____ $10 - 3 =$ _____

$8 - 7 =$ _____ $5 - 4 =$ _____ $7 - 2 =$ _____

$10 - 8 =$ _____ $6 - 5 =$ _____ $8 - 6 =$ _____

$5 - 3 =$ _____ $9 - 7 =$ _____ $10 - 1 =$ _____

$6 - 1 =$ _____ $8 - 4 =$ _____ $7 - 5 =$ _____

Week 4 **Practice Page 1**

10 – 6 = _____   9 – 5 = _____   10 – 7 = _____

8 – 5 = _____   9 – 6 = _____   10 – 5 = _____

6 – 4 = _____   7 – 3 = _____   4 – 1 = _____

10 – 3 = _____   10 – 9 = _____   7 – 4 = _____

7 – 6 = _____   6 – 2 = _____   4 – 3 = _____

5 – 2 = _____   9 – 4 = _____   10 – 1 = _____

7 – 1 = _____   8 – 6 = _____   10 – 8 = _____

9 – 3 = _____   5 – 4 = _____   8 – 2 = _____

Week 4   Practice Page 2

9 – 6 = _____   10 – 5 = _____   8 – 5 = _____

10 – 7 = _____   9 – 5 = _____   10 – 6 = _____

6 – 5 = _____   8 – 4 _____   9 – 1 = _____

8 – 3 = _____   9 – 7 = _____   6 – 3 = _____

7 – 2 = _____   4 – 2 = _____   10 – 2 = _____

8 – 7 = _____   8 – 1 = _____   9 – 8 = _____

9 – 2 = _____   5 – 1 = _____   3 – 1 = _____

6 – 1 = _____   5 – 3 = _____   10 – 4 = _____

Week 4   **Practice Page 3**

$8 - 3 =$ _____ $9 - 6 =$ _____ $8 - 1 =$ _____

$7 - 2 =$ _____ $10 - 7 =$ _____ $10 - 4 =$ _____

$8 - 7 =$ _____ $6 - 5 =$ _____ $9 - 1 =$ _____

$9 - 7 =$ _____ $10 - 5 =$ _____ $6 - 3 =$ _____

$4 - 2 =$ _____ $9 - 5 =$ _____ $10 - 2 =$ _____

$8 - 5 =$ _____ $8 - 4 =$ _____ $9 - 8 =$ _____

$5 - 1 =$ _____ $9 - 2 =$ _____ $3 - 1 =$ _____

$5 - 3 =$ _____ $6 - 1 =$ _____ $10 - 6 =$ _____

Week 4   Practice Page 4

$10 - 1 =$ _____ $9 - 4 =$ _____ $10 - 3 =$ _____

$10 - 5 =$ _____ $9 - 3 =$ _____ $8 - 2 =$ _____

$4 - 1 =$ _____ $7 - 3 =$ _____ $6 - 4 =$ _____

$7 - 4 =$ _____ $10 - 9 =$ _____ $10 - 6 =$ _____

$4 - 3 =$ _____ $6 - 2 =$ _____ $7 - 6 =$ _____

$10 - 7 =$ _____ $9 - 5 =$ _____ $5 - 2 =$ _____

$10 - 8 =$ _____ $8 - 6 =$ _____ $7 - 1 =$ _____

$8 - 5 =$ _____ $5 - 4 =$ _____ $9 - 6 =$ _____

Week 5   **Practice Page 1**

11 – 9 = _____   13 – 9 = _____   16 – 9 = _____

14 – 9 = _____   18 – 9 = _____   12 – 9 = _____

15 – 9 = _____   17 – 9 = _____   10 – 7 = _____

8 – 5 = _____   6 – 4 = _____   8 – 4 = _____

10 – 6 = _____   9 – 2 = _____   9 – 5 = _____

6 – 3 = _____   6 – 1 = _____   7 – 6 = _____

6 – 2 = _____   9 – 6 = _____   2 – 1 = _____

5 – 3 = _____   10 – 1 = _____   10 – 5 = _____

Week 5   **Practice Page 2**

$12 - 9 =$ _____ $17 - 9 =$ _____ $16 - 9 =$ _____

$18 - 9 =$ _____ $14 - 9 =$ _____ $11 - 9 =$ _____

$15 - 9 =$ _____ $13 - 9 =$ _____ $10 - 8 =$ _____

$8 - 7 =$ _____ $5 - 4 =$ _____ $10 - 2 =$ _____

$6 - 5 =$ _____ $5 - 2 =$ _____ $8 - 6 =$ _____

$10 - 9 =$ _____ $7 - 3 =$ _____ $5 - 1 =$ _____

$9 - 7 =$ _____ $4 - 3 =$ _____ $9 - 1 =$ _____

$7 - 5 =$ _____ $9 - 3 =$ _____ $9 - 8 =$ _____

Week 5   **Practice Page 3**

$7 - 4 =$ _____ $8 - 1 =$ _____ $13 - 9 =$ _____

$4 - 2 =$ _____ $16 - 9 =$ _____ $4 - 1 =$ _____

$10 - 7 =$ _____ $15 - 9 =$ _____ $17 - 9 =$ _____

$11 - 9 =$ _____ $8 - 5 =$ _____ $6 - 4 =$ _____

$9 - 5 =$ _____ $10 - 6 =$ _____ $9 - 4 =$ _____

$7 - 6 =$ _____ $18 - 9 =$ _____ $14 - 9 =$ _____

$3 - 2 =$ _____ $7 - 2 =$ _____ $9 - 6 =$ _____

$10 - 5 =$ _____ $5 - 3 =$ _____ $12 - 9 =$ _____

Week 5   **Practice Page 4**

$16 - 9 =$ _____ $8 - 3 =$ _____ $17 - 9 =$ _____

$11 - 9 =$ _____ $3 - 1 =$ _____ $10 - 3 =$ _____

$10 - 8 =$ _____ $9 - 8 =$ _____ $8 - 6 =$ _____

$14 - 9 =$ _____ $8 - 7 =$ _____ $5 - 4 =$ _____

$13 - 9 =$ _____ $6 - 5 =$ _____ $8 - 2 =$ _____

$10 - 4 =$ _____ $10 - 9 =$ _____ $12 - 9 =$ _____

$7 - 1 =$ _____ $9 - 7 =$ _____ $18 - 9 =$ _____

$9 - 8 =$ _____ $7 - 5 =$ _____ $15 - 9 =$ _____

Week 6   Practice Page 1

$12 - 8 = \underline{\hspace{1.5cm}}$ $15 - 8 = \underline{\hspace{1.5cm}}$ $11 - 8 = \underline{\hspace{1.5cm}}$

$14 - 8 = \underline{\hspace{1.5cm}}$ $17 - 8 = \underline{\hspace{1.5cm}}$ $13 - 8 = \underline{\hspace{1.5cm}}$

$16 - 8 = \underline{\hspace{1.5cm}}$ $14 - 9 = \underline{\hspace{1.5cm}}$ $10 - 7 = \underline{\hspace{1.5cm}}$

$9 - 3 = \underline{\hspace{1.5cm}}$ $9 - 5 = \underline{\hspace{1.5cm}}$ $12 - 9 = \underline{\hspace{1.5cm}}$

$16 - 9 = \underline{\hspace{1.5cm}}$ $5 - 3 = \underline{\hspace{1.5cm}}$ $10 - 1 = \underline{\hspace{1.5cm}}$

$11 - 9 = \underline{\hspace{1.5cm}}$ $8 - 6 = \underline{\hspace{1.5cm}}$ $18 - 9 = \underline{\hspace{1.5cm}}$

$10 - 5 = \underline{\hspace{1.5cm}}$ $15 - 9 = \underline{\hspace{1.5cm}}$ $6 - 3 = \underline{\hspace{1.5cm}}$

$17 - 9 = \underline{\hspace{1.5cm}}$ $6 - 5 = \underline{\hspace{1.5cm}}$ $13 - 9 = \underline{\hspace{1.5cm}}$

Week 6   Practice Page 2

$11 - 8 =$ _____ $14 - 8 =$ _____ $16 - 8 =$ _____

$13 - 8 =$ _____ $15 - 8 =$ _____ $17 - 8 =$ _____

$12 - 8 =$ _____ $5 - 4 =$ _____ $15 - 9 =$ _____

$8 - 7 =$ _____ $10 - 2 =$ _____ $13 - 9$ _____

$14 - 9 =$ _____ $8 - 4 =$ _____ $18 - 9 =$ _____

$4 - 3 =$ _____ $11 - 9 =$ _____ $10 - 6 =$ _____

$7 - 6 =$ _____ $16 - 9 =$ _____ $8 - 5 =$ _____

$17 - 9 =$ _____ $9 - 6 =$ _____ $12 - 9 =$ _____

Week 6   Practice Page 3

$8 - 5 =$ _____ $11 - 8 =$ _____ $12 - 9 =$ _____

$9 - 8 =$ _____ $6 - 4 =$ _____ $16 - 8 =$ _____

$12 - 8 =$ _____ $10 - 6 =$ _____ $10 - 4 =$ _____

$15 - 8 =$ _____ $9 - 5 =$ _____ $13 - 8 =$ _____

$10 - 5 =$ _____ $13 - 9 =$ _____ $9 - 1 =$ _____

$7 - 4 =$ _____ $17 - 8 =$ _____ $10 - 7 =$ _____

$10 - 9 =$ _____ $10 - 3 =$ _____ $9 - 2 =$ _____

$11 - 9 =$ _____ $14 - 8 =$ _____ $9 - 6 =$ _____

Week 6   **Practice Page 4**

14 − 8 = _____   8 − 5 = _____   16 − 9 = _____

10 − 8 = _____   15 − 8 = _____   7 − 3 = _____

17 − 8 = _____   8 − 3 = _____   9 − 5 = _____

18 − 9 = _____   10 − 7 = _____   12 − 8 = _____

9 − 6 = _____   14 − 9 = _____   17 − 9 = _____

11 − 8 = _____   10 − 5 = _____   8 − 2 = _____

9 − 4 = _____   9 − 7 = _____   13 − 8 = _____

15 − 9 = _____   16 − 8 = _____   10 − 6 = _____

Week 7

Practice Page 1

$14 - 5 = $ _____ $11 - 4 = $ _____ $13 - 4 = $ _____

$11 - 2 = $ _____ $12 - 4 = $ _____ $11 - 5 = $ _____

$12 - 5 = $ _____ $11 - 3 = $ _____ $13 - 5 = $ _____

$12 - 3 = $ _____ $13 - 9 = $ _____ $10 - 6 = $ _____

$18 - 9 = $ _____ $8 - 6 = $ _____ $14 - 8 = $ _____

$12 - 9 = $ _____ $16 - 8 = $ _____ $8 - 5 = $ _____

$15 - 9 = $ _____ $9 - 6 = $ _____ $5 - 2 = $ _____

$11 - 8 = $ _____ $10 - 9 = $ _____ $17 - 9 = $ _____

Week 7   **Practice Page 2**

$12 - 5 =$ _____ $11 - 3 =$ _____ $13 - 5 =$ _____

$11 - 2 =$ _____ $12 - 3 =$ _____ $11 - 5 =$ _____

$14 - 5 =$ _____ $11 - 4 =$ _____ $13 - 4 =$ _____

$12 - 4 =$ _____ $10 - 8 =$ _____ $13 - 8 =$ _____

$10 - 5 =$ _____ $8 - 3 =$ _____ $17 - 8 =$ _____

$16 - 9 =$ _____ $12 - 8 =$ _____ $7 - 2 =$ _____

$7 - 6 =$ _____ $11 - 9 =$ _____ $9 - 5 =$ _____

$15 - 8 =$ _____ $10 - 7 =$ _____ $14 - 9 =$ _____

Week 7   **Practice Page 3**

$9 - 2 =$ _____ $10 - 7 =$ _____ $6 - 1 =$ _____

$11 - 8 =$ _____ $13 - 4 =$ _____ $16 - 8 =$ _____

$9 - 4 =$ _____ $11 - 5 =$ _____ $9 - 7 =$ _____

$10 - 6 =$ _____ $13 - 5 =$ _____ $12 - 8 =$ _____

$11 - 4 =$ _____ $14 - 8 =$ _____ $14 - 5 =$ _____

$12 - 4 =$ _____ $7 - 3 =$ _____ $11 - 2 =$ _____

$11 - 3 =$ _____ $7 - 4 =$ _____ $12 - 5 =$ _____

$8 - 1 =$ _____ $10 - 4 =$ _____ $12 - 3 =$ _____

Week 7   **Practice Page 4**

$13 - 8 =$ _____ $6 - 3 =$ _____ $13 - 5 =$ _____

$9 - 8 =$ _____ $17 - 8 =$ _____ $11 - 5 =$ _____

$10 - 3 =$ _____ $12 - 5 =$ _____ $13 - 4 =$ _____

$14 - 8 =$ _____ $11 - 2 =$ _____ $8 - 5 =$ _____

$10 - 5 =$ _____ $14 - 5 =$ _____ $9 - 3 =$ _____

$11 - 3 =$ _____ $12 - 4 =$ _____ $10 - 1 =$ _____

$12 - 3 =$ _____ $8 - 7 =$ _____ $9 - 6 =$ _____

$11 - 4 =$ _____ $9 - 5 =$ _____ $10 - 2 =$ _____

Week 8   **Practice Page 1**

16 − 7 = _____   11 − 6 = _____   12 − 7 = _____

13 − 7 = _____   14 − 7 = _____   15 − 6 = _____

12 − 6 = _____   11 − 7 = _____   13 − 6 = _____

14 − 6 = _____   15 − 7 = _____   12 − 3 = _____

12 − 5 = _____   11 − 8 = _____   13 − 8 = _____

11 − 4 = _____   14 − 5 = _____   11 − 3 = _____

12 − 8 = _____   12 − 4 = _____   11 − 5 = _____

13 − 4 = _____   11 − 2 = _____   13 − 5 = _____

Week 8   Practice Page 2

$11 - 6 =$ _____ $14 - 6 =$ _____ $16 - 7 =$ _____

$14 - 7 =$ _____ $12 - 7 =$ _____ $13 - 7 =$ _____

$11 - 7 =$ _____ $15 - 6 =$ _____ $12 - 6 =$ _____

$15 - 7 =$ _____ $13 - 6 =$ _____ $15 - 8 =$ _____

$11 - 2 =$ _____ $13 - 4 =$ _____ $12 - 5 =$ _____

$14 - 8 =$ _____ $16 - 8 =$ _____ $12 - 3 =$ _____

$17 - 8 =$ _____ $12 - 4 =$ _____ $13 - 5 =$ _____

$11 - 5 =$ _____ $14 - 5 =$ _____ $11 - 3 =$ _____

Week 8   **Practice Page 3**

$11 - 6 =$ _____ $12 - 7 =$ _____ $14 - 5 =$ _____

$12 - 3 =$ _____ $11 - 4 =$ _____ $13 - 6 =$ _____

$14 - 7 =$ _____ $13 - 5 =$ _____ $14 - 8 =$ _____

$16 - 9 =$ _____ $11 - 3 =$ _____ $15 - 7 =$ _____

$12 - 5 =$ _____ $12 - 6 =$ _____ $11 - 7 =$ _____

$15 - 6 =$ _____ $13 - 9 =$ _____ $13 - 4 =$ _____

$12 - 4 =$ _____ $16 - 7 =$ _____ $11 - 2 =$ _____

$13 - 7 =$ _____ $11 - 5 =$ _____ $14 - 6 =$ _____

Week 8   **Practice Page 4**

$11 - 2 = $ _____ $12 - 4 = $ _____ $14 - 7 = $ _____

$13 - 6 = $ _____ $12 - 5 = $ _____ $12 - 9 = $ _____

$15 - 7 = $ _____ $11 - 7 = $ _____ $15 - 9 = $ _____

$14 - 5 = $ _____ $11 - 3 = $ _____ $14 - 6 = $ _____

$12 - 7 = $ _____ $11 - 6 = $ _____ $13 - 4 = $ _____

$11 - 5 = $ _____ $16 - 7 = $ _____ $15 - 6 = $ _____

$12 - 6 = $ _____ $13 - 5 = $ _____ $12 - 3 = $ _____

$11 - 4 = $ _____ $13 - 7 = $ _____ $11 - 9 = $ _____

ANSWER KEYS

Week 1		Practice Page 1
9 – 2 = 7	4 – 1 = 3	6 – 1 = 5
5 – 2 = 3	7 – 1 = 6	6 – 2 = 4
10 – 1 = 9	3 – 1 = 2	9 – 2 = 7
5 – 1 = 4	7 – 2 = 5	8 – 1 = 7
8 – 2 = 6	3 – 2 = 1	2 – 1 = 1
4 – 2 = 2	9 – 1 = 8	10 – 2 = 8

Week 1		Practice Page 2
9 – 2 = 7	4 – 1 = 3	6 – 1 = 5
7 – 1 = 6	5 – 2 = 3	6 – 2 = 4
3 – 1 = 2	10 – 1 = 9	9 – 2 = 7
7 – 2 = 5	5 – 1 = 4	8 – 1 = 7
3 – 2 = 1	8 – 2 = 6	2 – 1 = 1
9 – 1 = 8	4 – 2 = 2	10 – 2 = 8

Week 1		Practice Page 3
3 – 1 = 2	10 – 1 = 9	9 – 2 = 7
7 – 2 = 5	5 – 1 = 4	8 – 1 = 7
3 – 2 = 1	8 – 2 = 6	2 – 1 = 1
9 – 1 = 8	4 – 2 = 2	10 – 2 = 8
9 – 2 = 7	4 – 1 = 3	6 – 1 = 5
7 – 1 = 6	5 – 2 = 3	6 – 2 = 4

Week 1		Practice Page 4
10 – 1 = 9	3 – 1 = 2	9 – 2 = 7
5 – 1 = 4	7 – 2 = 5	8 – 1 = 7
8 – 2 = 6	3 – 2 = 1	2 – 1 = 1
4 – 2 = 2	9 – 1 = 8	10 – 2 = 8
4 – 1 = 3	9 – 2 = 7	6 – 1 = 5
5 – 2 = 3	7 – 1 = 6	6 – 2 = 4

Week 2		Practice Page 1
8 − 3 = 5	3 − 2 = 1	9 − 4 = 5
2 − 1 = 1	7 − 3 = 4	9 − 1 = 8
5 − 2 = 3	10 − 3 = 7	8 − 2 = 6
8 − 4 = 4	8 − 2 = 6	3 − 1 = 2
7 − 2 = 5	7 − 4 = 3	9 − 3 = 6
10 − 4 = 6	6 − 1 = 5	6 − 3 = 3

Week 2		Practice Page 2
8 − 4 = 4	9 − 2 = 7	8 − 1 = 7
10 − 2 = 8	7 − 4 = 3	9 − 3 = 6
10 − 4 = 6	5 − 1 = 4	6 − 3 = 3
8 − 3 = 5	6 − 2 = 4	9 − 4 = 5
4 − 2 = 2	7 − 3 = 4	10 − 1 = 9
4 − 1 = 3	10 − 3 = 7	7 − 1 = 6

Week 2		Practice Page 3
10 − 1 = 9	8 − 2 = 6	8 − 4 = 4
7 − 4 = 3	9 − 3 = 6	3 − 1 = 2
4 − 2 = 2	6 − 3 = 3	10 − 4 = 6
6 − 1 = 5	9 − 4 = 5	8 − 3 = 5
7 − 3 = 4	7 − 2 = 5	5 − 2 = 3
10 − 3 = 7	7 − 1 = 6	9 − 2 = 7

Week 2		Practice Page 4
10 − 2 = 8	6 − 3 = 3	10 − 4 = 6
5 − 1 = 4	9 − 4 = 5	8 − 3 = 5
9 − 1 = 8	6 − 2 = 4	8 − 4 = 4
7 − 4 = 3	9 − 3 = 6	7 − 2 = 5
7 − 3 = 4	2 − 1 = 1	4 − 1 = 3
10 − 3 = 7	8 − 1 = 7	3 − 2 = 1

Week 3   Practice Page 1

6 − 5 = 1   8 − 6 = 2   10 − 8 = 2

9 − 7 = 2   10 − 2 = 8   5 − 3 = 2

5 − 2 = 3   7 − 5 = 2   9 − 3 = 6

7 − 6 = 1   8 − 3 = 5   6 − 4 = 2

10 − 3 = 7   10 − 9 = 1   4 − 3 = 1

9 − 8 = 1   7 − 3 = 4   4 − 1 = 3

5 − 4 = 1   8 − 1 = 7   8 − 7 = 1

Week 3   Practice Page 2

10 − 8 = 2   6 − 5 = 1   8 − 6 = 2

5 − 3 = 2   9 − 7 = 2   7 − 4 = 3

6 − 2 = 4   9 − 4 = 5   7 − 5 = 2

6 − 4 = 2   7 − 6 = 1   7 − 1 = 6

4 − 3 = 1   9 − 2 = 7   10 − 9 = 1

10 − 4 = 6   9 − 8 = 1   8 − 4 = 4

8 − 7 = 1   5 − 4 = 1   6 − 3 = 3

Week 3   Practice Page 3

4 − 3 = 1   6 − 3 = 3   10 − 9 = 1

7 − 4 = 3   9 − 8 = 1   9 − 4 = 5

8 − 7 = 1   5 − 4 = 1   8 − 2 = 6

10 − 8 = 2   6 − 5 = 1   8 − 6 = 2

5 − 3 = 2   9 − 7 = 2   5 − 1 = 4

9 − 1 = 8   8 − 3 = 5   7 − 5 = 2

6 − 4 = 2   7 − 6 = 1   10 − 4 = 6

Week 3   Practice Page 4

6 − 4 = 2   7 − 6 = 1   4 − 2 = 2

4 − 3 = 1   7 − 3 = 4   10 − 9 = 1

9 − 3 = 6   9 − 8 = 1   10 − 3 = 7

8 − 7 = 1   5 − 4 = 1   7 − 2 = 5

10 − 8 = 2   6 − 5 = 1   8 − 6 = 2

5 − 3 = 2   9 − 7 = 2   10 − 1 = 9

6 − 1 = 5   8 − 4 = 4   7 − 5 = 2

Week 4		Practice Page 1
10 − 6 = 4	9 − 5 = 4	10 − 7 = 3
8 − 5 = 3	9 − 6 = 3	10 − 5 = 5
6 − 4 = 2	7 − 3 = 4	4 − 1 = 3
10 − 3 = 7	10 − 9 = 1	7 − 4 = 3
7 − 6 = 1	6 − 2 = 4	4 − 3 = 1
5 − 2 = 3	9 − 4 = 5	10 − 1 = 9
7 − 1 = 6	8 − 6 = 2	10 − 8 = 2
9 − 3 = 6	5 − 4 = 1	8 − 2 = 6

Week 4		Practice Page 2
9 − 6 = 3	10 − 5 = 5	8 − 5 = 3
10 − 7 = 3	9 − 5 = 4	10 − 6 = 4
6 − 5 = 1	8 − 4 = 4	9 − 1 = 8
8 − 3 = 5	9 − 7 = 2	6 − 3 = 3
7 − 2 = 5	4 − 2 = 2	10 − 2 = 8
8 − 7 = 1	8 − 1 = 7	9 − 8 = 1
9 − 2 = 7	5 − 1 = 4	3 − 1 = 2
6 − 1 = 5	5 − 3 = 2	10 − 4 = 6

Week 4		Practice Page 3
8 − 3 = 5	9 − 6 = 3	8 − 1 = 7
7 − 2 = 5	10 − 7 = 3	10 − 4 = 6
8 − 7 = 1	6 − 5 = 1	9 − 1 = 8
9 − 7 = 2	10 − 5 = 5	6 − 3 = 3
4 − 2 = 2	9 − 5 = 4	10 − 2 = 8
8 − 5 = 3	8 − 4 = 4	9 − 8 = 1
5 − 1 = 4	9 − 2 = 7	3 − 1 = 2
5 − 3 = 2	6 − 1 = 5	10 − 6 = 4

Week 4		Practice Page 4
10 − 1 = 9	9 − 4 = 5	10 − 3 = 7
10 − 5 = 5	9 − 3 = 6	8 − 2 = 6
4 − 1 = 3	7 − 3 = 4	6 − 4 = 2
7 − 4 = 3	10 − 9 = 1	10 − 6 = 4
4 − 3 = 1	6 − 2 = 4	7 − 6 = 1
10 − 7 = 3	9 − 5 = 4	5 − 2 = 3
10 − 8 = 2	8 − 6 = 2	7 − 1 = 6
8 − 5 = 3	5 − 4 = 1	9 − 6 = 3

Week 5		Practice Page 1
11 – 9 = 2	13 – 9 = 4	16 – 9 = 7
14 – 9 = 5	18 – 9 = 9	12 – 9 = 3
15 – 9 = 6	17 – 9 = 8	10 – 7 = 3
8 – 5 = 3	6 – 4 = 2	8 – 4 = 4
10 – 6 = 4	9 – 2 = 7	9 – 5 = 4
6 – 3 = 3	6 – 1 = 5	7 – 6 = 1
6 – 2 = 4	9 – 6 = 3	2 – 1 = 1
5 – 3 = 2	10 – 1 = 9	10 – 5 = 5

Week 5		Practice Page 2
12 – 9 = 3	17 – 9 = 8	16 – 9 = 7
18 – 9 = 9	14 – 9 = 5	11 – 9 = 2
15 – 9 = 6	13 – 9 = 4	10 – 8 = 2
8 – 7 = 1	5 – 4 = 1	10 – 2 = 8
6 – 5 = 1	5 – 2 = 3	8 – 6 = 2
10 – 9 = 1	7 – 3 = 4	5 – 1 = 4
9 – 7 = 2	4 – 3 = 1	9 – 1 = 8
7 – 5 = 2	9 – 3 = 6	9 – 8 = 1

Week 5		Practice Page 3
7 – 4 = 3	8 – 1 = 7	13 – 9 = 4
4 – 2 = 2	16 – 9 = 7	4 – 1 = 3
10 – 7 = 3	15 – 9 = 6	17 – 9 = 8
11 – 9 = 2	8 – 5 = 3	6 – 4 = 2
9 – 5 = 4	10 – 6 = 4	9 – 4 = 5
7 – 6 = 1	18 – 9 = 9	14 – 9 = 5
3 – 2 = 1	7 – 2 = 5	9 – 6 = 3
10 – 5 = 5	5 – 3 = 2	12 – 9 = 3

Week 5		Practice Page 4
16 – 9 = 7	8 – 3 = 5	17 – 9 = 8
11 – 9 = 2	3 – 1 = 2	10 – 3 = 7
10 – 8 = 2	9 – 8 = 1	8 – 6 = 2
14 – 9 = 5	8 – 7 = 1	5 – 4 = 1
13 – 9 = 4	6 – 5 = 1	8 – 2 = 6
10 – 4 = 6	10 – 9 = 1	12 – 9 = 3
7 – 1 = 6	9 – 7 = 2	18 – 9 = 9
9 – 8 = 1	7 – 5 = 2	15 – 9 = 6

Week 6		Practice Page 1
12 − 8 = 4	15 − 8 = 7	11 − 8 = 3
14 − 8 = 6	17 − 8 = 9	13 − 8 = 5
16 − 8 = 8	14 − 9 = 5	10 − 7 = 3
9 − 3 = 6	9 − 5 = 4	12 − 9 = 3
16 − 9 = 7	5 − 3 = 2	10 − 1 = 9
11 − 9 = 2	8 − 6 = 2	18 − 9 = 9
10 − 5 = 5	15 − 9 = 6	6 − 3 = 3
17 − 9 = 8	6 − 5 = 1	13 − 9 = 4

Week 6		Practice Page 2
11 − 8 = 3	14 − 8 = 6	16 − 8 = 8
13 − 8 = 5	15 − 8 = 7	17 − 8 = 9
12 − 8 = 4	5 − 4 = 1	15 − 9 = 6
8 − 7 = 1	10 − 2 = 8	13 − 9 = 4
14 − 9 = 5	8 − 4 = 4	18 − 9 = 9
4 − 3 = 1	11 − 9 = 2	10 − 6 = 4
7 − 6 = 1	16 − 9 = 7	8 − 5 = 3
17 − 9 = 8	9 − 6 = 3	12 − 9 = 3

Week 6		Practice Page 3
8 − 5 = 3	11 − 8 = 3	12 − 9 = 3
9 − 8 = 1	6 − 4 = 2	16 − 8 = 8
12 − 8 = 4	10 − 6 = 4	10 − 4 = 6
15 − 8 = 7	9 − 5 = 4	13 − 8 = 5
10 − 5 = 5	13 − 9 = 4	9 − 1 = 8
7 − 4 = 3	17 − 8 = 9	10 − 7 = 3
10 − 9 = 1	10 − 3 = 7	9 − 2 = 7
11 − 9 = 2	14 − 8 = 6	9 − 6 = 3

Week 6		Practice Page 4
14 − 8 = 6	8 − 5 = 3	16 − 9 = 7
10 − 8 = 2	15 − 8 = 7	7 − 3 = 4
17 − 8 = 9	8 − 3 = 5	9 − 5 = 4
18 − 9 = 9	10 − 7 = 3	12 − 8 = 4
9 − 6 = 3	14 − 9 = 5	17 − 9 = 8
11 − 8 = 3	10 − 5 = 5	8 − 2 = 6
9 − 4 = 5	9 − 7 = 2	13 − 8 = 5
15 − 9 = 6	16 − 8 = 8	10 − 6 = 4

Week 7		Practice Page 1
14 – 5 = 9	11 – 4 = 7	13 – 4 = 9
11 – 2 = 9	12 – 4 = 8	11 – 5 = 6
12 – 5 = 7	11 – 3 = 8	13 – 5 = 8
12 – 3 = 9	13 – 9 = 4	10 – 6 = 4
18 – 9 = 9	8 – 6 = 2	14 – 8 = 6
12 – 9 = 3	16 – 8 = 8	8 – 5 = 3
15 – 9 = 6	9 – 6 = 3	5 – 2 = 3
11 – 8 = 3	10 – 9 = 1	17 – 9 = 8

Week 7		Practice Page 2
12 – 5 = 7	11 – 3 = 8	13 – 5 = 8
11 – 2 = 9	12 – 3 = 9	11 – 5 = 6
14 – 5 = 9	11 – 4 = 7	13 – 4 = 9
12 – 4 = 8	10 – 8 = 2	13 – 8 = 5
10 – 5 = 5	8 – 3 = 5	17 – 8 = 9
16 – 9 = 7	12 – 8 = 4	7 – 2 = 5
7 – 6 = 1	11 – 9 = 2	9 – 5 = 4
15 – 8 = 7	10 – 7 = 3	14 – 9 = 5

Week 7		Practice Page 3
9 – 2 = 7	10 – 7 = 3	6 – 1 = 5
11 – 8 = 3	13 – 4 = 9	16 – 8 = 8
9 – 4 = 5	11 – 5 = 6	9 – 7 = 2
10 – 6 = 4	13 – 5 = 8	12 – 8 = 4
11 – 4 = 7	14 – 8 = 6	14 – 5 = 9
12 – 4 = 8	7 – 3 = 4	11 – 2 = 9
11 – 3 = 8	7 – 4 = 3	12 – 5 = 7
8 – 1 = 7	10 – 4 = 6	12 – 3 = 9

Week 7		Practice Page 4
13 – 8 = 5	6 – 3 = 3	13 – 5 = 8
9 – 8 = 1	17 – 8 = 9	11 – 5 = 6
10 – 3 = 7	12 – 5 = 7	13 – 4 = 9
14 – 8 = 6	11 – 2 = 9	8 – 5 = 3
10 – 5 = 5	14 – 5 = 9	9 – 3 = 6
11 – 3 = 8	12 – 4 = 8	10 – 1 = 9
12 – 3 = 9	8 – 7 = 1	9 – 6 = 3
11 – 4 = 7	9 – 5 = 4	10 – 2 = 8

Week 8		Practice Page 1
16 − 7 = 9	11 − 6 = 5	12 − 7 = 5
13 − 7 = 6	14 − 7 = 7	15 − 6 = 9
12 − 6 = 6	11 − 7 = 4	13 − 6 = 7
14 − 6 = 8	15 − 7 = 8	12 − 3 = 9
12 − 5 = 7	11 − 8 = 3	13 − 8 = 5
11 − 4 = 7	14 − 5 = 9	11 − 3 = 8
12 − 8 = 4	12 − 4 = 8	11 − 5 = 6
13 − 4 = 9	11 − 2 = 9	13 − 5 = 8

Week 8		Practice Page 2
11 − 6 = 5	14 − 6 = 8	16 − 7 = 9
14 − 7 = 7	12 − 7 = 5	13 − 7 = 6
11 − 7 = 4	15 − 6 = 9	12 − 6 = 6
15 − 7 = 8	13 − 6 = 7	15 − 8 = 7
11 − 2 = 9	13 − 4 = 9	12 − 5 = 7
14 − 8 = 6	16 − 8 = 8	12 − 3 = 9
17 − 8 = 9	12 − 4 = 8	13 − 5 = 8
11 − 5 = 6	14 − 5 = 9	11 − 3 = 8

Week 8		Practice Page 3
11 − 6 = 5	12 − 7 = 5	14 − 5 = 9
12 − 3 = 9	11 − 4 = 7	13 − 6 = 7
14 − 7 = 7	13 − 5 = 8	14 − 8 = 6
16 − 9 = 7	11 − 3 = 8	15 − 7 = 8
12 − 5 = 7	12 − 6 = 6	11 − 7 = 4
15 − 6 = 9	13 − 9 = 4	13 − 4 = 9
12 − 4 = 8	16 − 7 = 9	11 − 2 = 9
13 − 7 = 6	11 − 5 = 6	14 − 6 = 8

Week 8		Practice Page 4
11 − 2 = 9	12 − 4 = 8	14 − 7 = 7
13 − 6 = 7	12 − 5 = 7	12 − 9 = 3
15 − 7 = 8	11 − 7 = 4	15 − 9 = 6
14 − 5 = 9	11 − 3 = 8	14 − 6 = 8
12 − 7 = 5	11 − 6 = 5	13 − 4 = 9
11 − 5 = 6	16 − 7 = 9	15 − 6 = 9
12 − 6 = 6	13 − 5 = 8	12 − 3 = 9
11 − 4 = 7	13 − 7 = 6	11 − 9 = 2